My Experiments With Bad Poetry

Please don't read this

Syed Adil Husain

BookLeaf Publishing

India | USA | UK

Made with ❤ on the BookLeaf Publishing Platform
www.bookleafpub.in
www.bookleafpub.com

Dedication

To all the people who've called me a bad poet, you were right and I'm shameless.

Here are 21 more reasons why I shouldn't quit my job and become a full-time writer.

Preface

Please don't judge my grammar or my metaphors. They're going to be horrible—I know it, you know it, and yet, here we are.

I promise, I'm even worse at writing emails.

Have you ever heard of the word zilch? That's exactly how high your expectations should be as you read this.

This book isn't about great poetry. It's about writing anyway. It's about experimenting, failing, and sometimes —accidentally—stumbling onto something half-decent. But mostly, it's just about proving that bad poetry is still poetry and that I'm shameless enough to share it.

So, welcome. I'd tell you to enjoy, but let's not get ahead of ourselves.

Acknowledgements

Honestly, **I wouldn't change a thing.** But if you wanted **one tiny tweak**, maybe something like:

> **There's nothing to acknowledge.**

> But if I had to, I'd acknowledge **ChatGPT** for keeping me motivated enough to write... whatever this is.

> Also, I promise this isn't AI-generated. Look at how stunted the sentences are.

Either way, **this is golden.** Do you want to keep it as is, or do you feel like tweaking anything?

Uno. Starting something terrible

I wrote my first poem at nine
it was my grandfather's birthday
everybody said it's "good" and I
buried my head into a dictionary
not knowing what mockery is
but learnt what patronizing was
we had a garden in the verandah
I watched it from the side of my eye
face half-buried inside the dictionary
the money plant leaves shrank
from bright green to pale yellow
the mayflower bloomed like
a toilet cleaning plastic brush
the Hauz evaporated in seconds
only slippery green moss was left
my dreams slipped and tumbled
onto the dead freshwater fish
my poem became my taweez
but it never protected me
only begged for its protection
I wrote another and it was bad
I wrote another and it was worse
I wrote another that was the worst

then I stood first in third grade
and fourth grade
and fifth grade
and sixth grade
and seventh grade
and eighth grade
and everyone was happy.

Dos. English

My father never taught me English
but I had heard him speak
he sounded fluent like
the smoke from an expensive cigar
I have to use a thesaurus to
determine the synonyms of fluent
articulate
eloquent
silver-tongued
glib
cogent
I could've saved twenty seconds but
my father never taught me English
he was silver-tongued but
I taught myself Chemistry
no wonder his silver tongue
turned black like silver sulfide
whenever he spoke to me
or maybe it was the cheap
sugar with added sulfur
I guess we'll never know.

Tres. Love in the time of Libyan truck drivers

My family tree is
the Tree of Ténéré

no I cannot pronounce that

located in Niger's Sahara desert
it was considered the most isolated
tree on Earth and was tragically
run over by a Libyan truck driver
in 1973
snapping its trunk due to its
solitary position with no other
obstacles for miles around

now I wish I was struck by lightning
for trying to make poetry out of
a Googled statement

My love for you is bigger than Sahara
please be my Libyan truck driver
you can run me over and
end my bloodline
I don't even want kids

you don't even have to be drunk
but I hope you know how to
drive a truck on a desert road.

Quatro. Like Like Like!

Will you like me
like dust likes my
gaming laptop
like the word like likes
filling my vocabulary
like the stress gummy
likes my anxiety
like I like metaphors
like you like meteors
like you like light
polluting the sky
like you like
Times Square
like your hair
likes my notebooks
like your fingers like
intertwining
will you like me
like I like you.

Cinco. Urvashi Rautela

Texting you at 3 AM
with night mode on
a constant yawn
makes me wonder if
I'm Urvashi Rautela
because you're going to
forget our 2-month anniversary
because the light pollution
has destroyed your sleep
you're bad at pulling out
pulling yourselves together
pulling all-nighters and
bad at lying how your phone
always falls on your face
and knocks you off to sleep
I hope I'm not Urvashi Rautela
I know you've blocked her reels.

Seis. Mr. and Mrs. Sisyphus

Are you Times Square? because
I'm feeling fiscally irresponsible
I've increased the credit limits
of what my heart can take
I can afford luxury and
I just got a promotion
you're stuck in my head like
a cigarette advert jingle
an opioid pill billboard
a liquor commercial disguised
as sparkling mountain water
my eye sockets are flooded
with your lustre and radiance
your memory is a strobe light
Are you Times Square?
I want to spend the rest
of my light with you.

We can be impulsive together
we can amuse ourselves
to death together
we can be Mr and Mrs
Sisyphus and roll the
stones of workaholism up

along the mountains of debt
and imagine happiness forever.

Please be Times Square!
my mother wants me
to get married.

Siete. Pseudopodia

The pseudopodia on
the euglena diagram in
my biology notebook and
your biology notebook
are soaked with sweat
my forearm stinks of graphite
my fingers stink of pencil wood
you said you'd respond
to my love letter but
you only smirked like
that horror movie and
it's 3 AM and I'm scared
you could've just said no
I've wasted 3 hours
on your homework.

Ocho. COVID-19

Help me
I can't breathe
you gave me butterflies
that are writhing madly
inside my lungs
you said your kiss
would heal my heart
but I can't taste that
fake paneer pakoda
soaked in palm oil
from the cloud kitchen that
failed food safety tests
and gave me food poisoning
my weakness was my gut
but now it's my breath
I'm taking deep breaths
as if I had anxiety and
the therapist promised
it would go away if
I did fogging breaths
but I have brain fog now
at least make me that tea
that you said would calm me
at least book some oxygen

in the black market
at least pretend that
it's your fault
help me
I want to breathe
I'll write better poems if
you get me a ventilator
and an air-conditioned room
in a private hospital
I'll write poems for you until
the black market runs out
of oxygen cylinders
I'll write poems so bad
that even chatGPT
cannot replicate them
promise me
I want to live.

Nueve. Do you know a good psychiatrist?

I canceled my flight today
and missed the new one
because we had to meet
I saw you dancing
in that public garden
the summer heatwave
turned into such a spring
that I ended up with allergies
I sneezed and sneezed until
you said you'll bless me
the lilacs and daisies smirked
the butterflies sneered and
the imported red roses judged
with their imported water drips
covered in imported green moss
the imported chocolate that you
said was from a Welsh chocolatier
melted into the lines of my palm
and the palm reader said
my future was brown and
you laughed like it was a joke
I laughed like it was a joke
we laughed and you said

you're getting married soon
I missed my flight again like
I've missed you all this time
I went to the wrong terminal
I've grown tardy and all
that I can do now is smile
till my jaws bury my anxiety
do you know a good psychiatrist?

Diez. Waiting for a power-cut

You said you loved me enough
to alter my brain chemistry
the anxiety meds have calmed me
I want to feel butterflies swirl
inside my stomach until
my appendix bursts
I want my gut to writhe
with lactose intolerance
You said you'll love me more
than the stars in your telescope
more than the well-lit IT parks
more than the night shifts
more than your last-minutes
more than cold-brewed pour over
more than four cheese pizza
more than everything else
but you're in another galaxy
the night is soaked in skyglow
my circadian rhythm is gone and
tucked inside a blanket of light
so I wait for a power-cut
or a solar storm and wish
we did not discover fire.

Once. Mud and Baby Powder

You smelt like mud
when the rain stopped
the brown puddle water
I would float boats in
the red mosaic clay tiles
when they were soaked
the freshly painted walls
the sweet gum oozing
from the lemon tree's bark
the green algal growth
after a dark monsoon
the hummingbird feathers
stuck in red bottle brush
the grey cement tiles that
lay on my terrace and
you smelt like hope and
childhood and baby powder
and chrysanthemums and
the rope swing that hung
from that tamarind tree
near my father's house
that will never be a home
we were star-crossed lovers

in a Xavier Dolan movie
it was in all the film festivals
but then I got a bad cold
my nose is blocked and
I know you don't love me.

Doce. Bibi ka Maqbara

Do you remember the
red basalt maqbara
you promised you'd build
you said its skin would
erode to vantablack
it would vanish at night
they are reconstructing it
it's a world heritage site
with streets and streetlights
and dead moths and flies
can you come back and
dissolve the government's
archaeology department
maybe a little corruption
so that we can immigrate
to a country that would
accept our identity but
never consider us citizens.

Trece. Aurangabad

My family visited Aurangabad
I don't remember
how we got there
I can't remember when
it was a summer vacation
before global warming
smartphones with their
yellow light night modes
did not exist and I could
sleep my anxiety away
but the hotel rooms had
a glow in the dark ceiling
the city changed its name
I no longer talk to my father
but will you stick the stars
up on my off-white ceiling
before you leave me ravaged
like Aurangzeb on a rampage
I don't sleep without the lights on
since you told me about jinns.

Catorce. Peter Cat Recording Company

Would you come with me please
to that Western Ghat concert of
Peter Cat Recording Company
I promise we'll post stories
and get stuck in a landslide
amidst the worst monsoon ever
you can use that as a prompt
for your next journal entry
I promise I'm not anxious
about you publishing all of
your streams of consciousness
the blue pills are just mints
I promise I'll support you when
you're famous enough to
abandon me completely
let's just go, I really like
Peter Cat Recording Company.

Quince. Tardigrades

You and I are tardigrades
can I ask Elon Musk
to launch us to Mars
maybe that'll bring us
the spark you keep
yapping about.

Dieciséis. Breakfast

You had said I wouldn't
do anything for you

I'd return to office for you
start at 10 AM sharp
watch you eat unhealthy
sugar-coated corn flakes
while our future hollowed
itself like the cavities that
would've seethed in
our smiling white teeth

but you left because
you hated existential crises
and excel shortcuts

anyway

boiled eggs with pepper
are a healthier breakfast
and you were vegetarian.

Diecisiete. Do you have dental insurance?

Remember the toothpaste
you didn't prefer using
because it had microplastics,
synthetic menthol crystals,
and you didn't want
your mouth on fire.

I've changed it.

I even use a bamboo toothbrush
with herbal organic toothpaste.
It tastes like the fennel seeds
from that obscure farmer's market
in your hometown.

Please come back.

We could go for
teeth whitening together.
I have dental insurance,
and the new toothpaste
doesn't even work.

Dieciocho. Jesus of Suburbia

Long early morning walks
on the gravel-covered path
beside my old apartment.

We loved stumbling—
because nobody saw us.
The cement mixers,
the brokers,
the cigarette sellers—
they hadn't started their day.

I'm sorry that path
is now an asphalt road,
and the apartment complex
has become a housing society.

Don't worry.
Someday, when we've
found work-life balance,
and our parents haven't
moved in with us,

we'll find another
underdeveloped suburb

to finish what we started
and blare Jesus of Suburbia
in a flat we own.

Diecinueve. Diabetes

My refrigerator says
you are a liar
you said you didn't like
double chocolate cake
because it has sugar and
that is white poison
but I saw you sipping
a triple caramel syrup
whipped cream loaded
frappe in the coffee shop
where we first met
you should've picked
another place
am I not indulgent enough?
next time please don't leave
the fridge door open
the fridge magnet has
a hidden camera that takes
a snapshot of your soul.

Veinte. Slyvai Palth

Seven years ago, I read
about Sylvia Plath.
She took her own life
at the age of 30 by sealing
the kitchen of her London flat
with wet towels and cloths, then
placing her head in the oven
and turning on the gas.

Immediately, I turned to
an unbound and dilapidated
tenth-standard English textbook.
Its pages were soaked with
index finger sweat,
diabetic Complan spills,
and lactose intolerance.
I sat on a rusty steel chair,
reading Mirror by Plath,
pretending to understand because
English was the only subject
I could ever imagine being good at,
and the only competition was
me vs. me eating figs.

My kitchen couldn't be sealed.
Small towns in central India
don't have any publishers
who'd publish posthumously,
don't have enough men
who'd prefer to be eaten like air.

Sometimes, survival demands
being at one's worst, and
bad rhymes juxtaposed
with awful grammar, lifted
from Wren and Martin exercises,
make for a perfect poem—
as long as you don't want to die.

Veintiuno. Bukowski

Charles Bukowski came
all over my dreams and
my language broke
like haleem wheat
I need to get tested
for fatty liver asap
and possibly STDs
and you need to be tested
for being so beautiful that
my jaw dropped low and
I need to see a dentist
your infectious laughter
makes me want to
gobble on haleem and
some antibiotics till I
miss my course and the
bacteria inside me
become drug-resistant
and I know I said I love you
but you said you'll love me
only if I stop writing
why do you hate my poems?
did I hate your pretentious
Indian American accent?